Introduction

This book introduces a totally **new idea** into t
by the modern cake decorator. It shows si
make cut out lace pieces **of any length**, w
LACE'. They can be quickly and easily a
graceful look, which, hitherto, could on
consuming methods. The basic idea was first published ... ...
book 'Sugarcraft'(1991), where the cut-outs were made individually.

The matching border idea uses the same cutouts, and can also be used as a base border or collar.

The technique also enables the decorator to quickly manoeuvre the lace into delightful spirals, whirls and drapes, which, previously, would have taken hours to plan and execute.

This book gives a few basic ideas for you to practice on, such as interleaving the lace with Garrett Frills.

The possible variations are endless, limited only by your imagination. Further designs of tools for the lace edging and cut-outs will be introduced shortly.

The Tools. General Notes:

Non-stick. One of their most useful aspects is their non-stick property, which is inherent in the design and material used. It is not a surface finish and, therefore, cannot wear off. It also means they cut cleanly, without fuzzy edges.

Materials. All the tools can be used with any soft material such as flowerpaste, sugarpaste, marzipan, modelling chocolate, plasticine, modelling clay etc.

Temperature. Normally hand washing in warm soapy water is all that is required. They will withstand boiling water or the dishwasher without deforming. A string bag is useful to reduce turbulence.

Handles. All the cutters have comfortably sized handles which allow you to exert firm pressure over the whole of the cutting edges.

Stability. They will not rust, corrode, deform or wear out with normal useage. They should not be scrubbed on the board or twisted.

Marking. All the tools are permanently marked to aid easy identification.

Metal.   The cutters are delicate and should not be brought into contact with sharp metal objects which may damage the cutting edges or surfaces. i.e.keep them separated from metal cutters.

Hygiene.   The materials meet the appropriate EEC regulations for food hygiene.

Endorsement. All the items are personally endorsed and used by PAT ASHBY, our Technical Director, who is one of the leading teachers of sugarcraft in the UK and is an International judge and demonstrator.

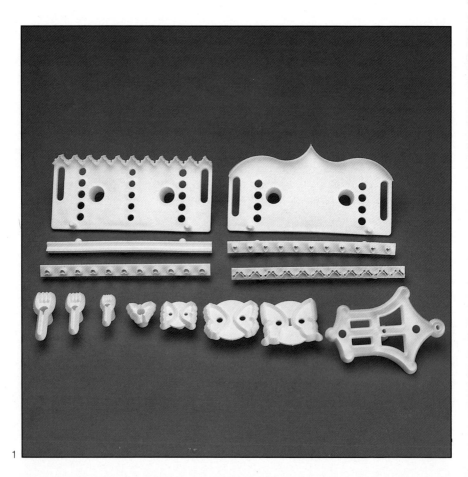

1

THE NEW CUTTERS *(See Illustration 1).*

(Full Size shapes are shown in Illustrations 2 & 3)

1. The Lace Cutter Body (LA1). This gives the basic 'lacey' edge and provides locations for the adjustable blades. It is endless, so that by moving the cutter along, any length of lace may be produced.

2. The Straight Blade (LA2A). This fits into any position on LA1(or LB1)to give a precise width to the piece of lace. It is NOT interchangeable with the Endless Garrett Frill Cutter Blade (EGF6).

3. The 'Heart' shaped cut out Blade (LA2B). This fits into any position on LA1 (or LB1) to cut out 11 heart shaped holes simultaneously. It can also be hand held to cut holes in any position. It is also available cut into 1, 2, 3 & 5 hole sets for hand held use.

Items 1,2 & 3 make up the basic Lace Cutter Set.

4. The 'Bean' shaped cut out Blade (LA2C). As for LA2B, but with 11 bean shaped holes.

5. The 'Two Dumbell' shaped cut out Blade (LA2D). As for LA2B, but with 11 two-dumbell shaped holes.

All the blades are available separately, so that multiple holes can be cut simultaneously.

6. The Border Body (LB1). This is used in exactly the same way as the Lace Cutter(LA1), providing a different edge shape, but using the same Blades so that the hole cutouts will match those in the Lace.

7. The Lantern Cutter (L1). This cutter can be used to cut out a shape to attach to the side or top of a cake, or emboss the outline on the surface of the cake, or make a three dimensional lantern as a centrepiece.

8. The Honeysuckle Cutter Set (HS1,HS2,HS3). These make honeysuckle flowers very easily, using the 'Mexican Hat' method.

9. The Butterfly Cutter Set (B1,B2,B3,B4). These cutters provide two matched wings for each size, and you pipe the body with Royal Icing.

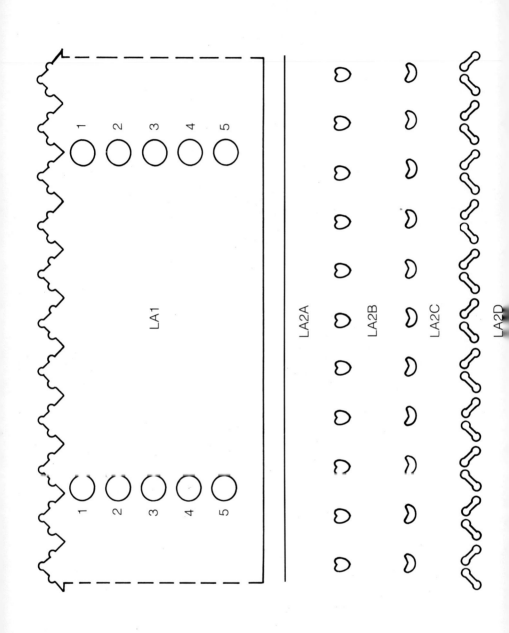

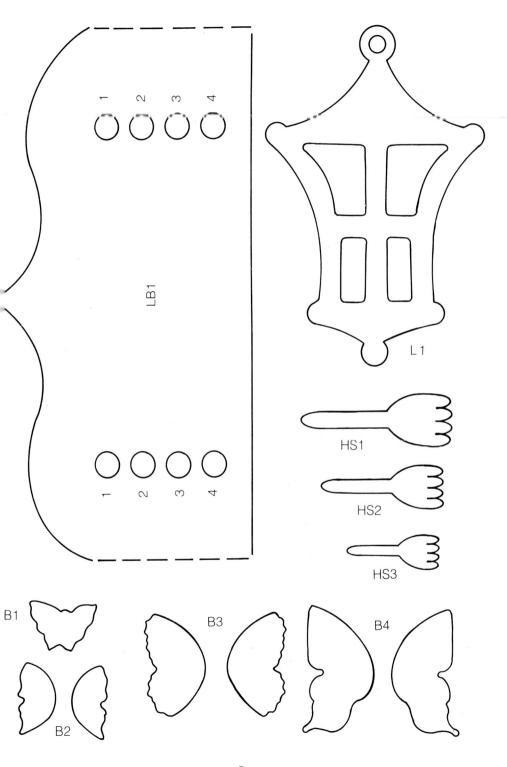

Materials for the Lace.

The lace can be made from many types of sugarpaste, flowerpaste or pastillage, but the commercial ones need some strengthening to make it easier to handle, by adding a small amount of Gum Trag.(See Recipes Pages 39/40).I have used the term 'lace paste' throughout this book to cover any of the pastes that you may wish to use. If you intend to use the lace to make structures – such as the wedding top – it is advisable to use pastillage for greater strength.

How to make the Lace pieces. (*See Illustrations 4 & 5*)

(A non-stick plastic board is almost essential for this operation).

Lace A. 1. Fit the Straight Blade (LA2A) into any of the holes numbered 2 to 5 in the Lace Body (LA1). This sets the width of the piece – from $^7/_8$ to $2^1/_8$ Then fit the 'Heart' blade (LA2B) inside the Straight Blade into any of the holes numbered 1 to 4.

2. Roll out the lace paste, not too thinly, and press the assembled cutter firmly onto the paste. **Run your fingers along the top of the cutter** to make sure the holes are all cut properly. **DO NOT** scrub or twist the cutter. Lift straight up and then, if a longer piece is required, move the cutter along, line up carefully with the previous cut and press down and lift up as before. Cut to the exact length required (the Straight Blade 1 (of 2) LA2A and makes an excellent knife) and peel away the surplus material.

NB: For ease of handling, strips of about 10 – 12" long are the most convenient. For longer pieces butt the ends of the strips together when applying to the cake.

3. Then lift the Lace piece off the board **with the cut-outs still in place***, moisten with a little water and attach to the cake in the required position. Carefully push out the cut-outs with a cocktail stick just before the paste begins to harden.

If you intend to stand it upright, use paste glue (see Page 40) for greater strength and an invisible join!

*This helps to reduce any tendency of the piece to distort or stretch.

NB: If any paste should stick in the 'hole' cutters, carefully push it out from the back. For the Two Dumbell Cutter (LA2D), use a strip of thin card or plastic to push out any reluctant pieces. It is easier and safer than using a pin.

Lace B. 1. For a finer lace, fit the Straight Blade (LA2A) into any of the holes 1 to 5 in the Lace Body (LA1). This sets the width of the piece. Do not fit the Heart Blade at this point.

2. Roll out the lace paste, not too thinly, and press the assembled cutter firmly onto the paste. DO NOT scrub or twist the cutter. Lift straight up and then, if a longer piece is required, move the cutter along, line up carefully with the previous cut and press down and lift up as before.

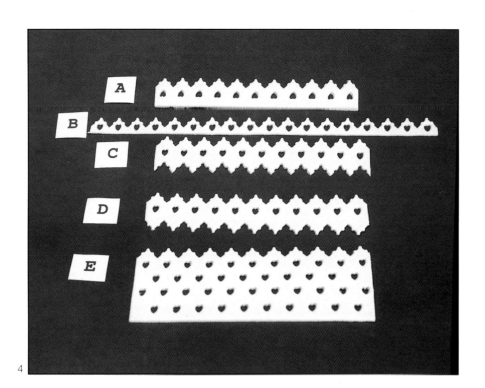

4

5

NB: For ease of handling, strips of about 10" – 12" long are the most convenient. For longer pieces butt the ends of the strips together when applying to the cake.

3. Now, holding the Heart Blade (LA2B) as close to the lacy edge of the cut-out piece as you can, press down and **run your finger along the top of the blade** to ensure all the holes are cut properly, then lift up. Cut to the exact length required and peel away the surplus material.

4. Proceed as for Step 3 of Lace A.

Lace C. 1. For lace with a 'lacy' edge on both sides, leave out the Straight Blade(LA2A) and, after Step 2 of Lace B, position the lacy edge of the Lace Body Cutter(LA1) a little below the holes you have just cut, and cut again.

For an attractive edging strip, leave out the holes. (*See Illustration 5*)

Lace D. As for Lace C, but turn LA1 round.

(Laces C and D are useful as a top edging since they give an upright **and** a hanging lace. See Illustration 31).

Lace E. 1. If several blades are fitted into **alternate** holes in LA1, and then further staggered holes cut by hand in between, then an attractive perforated drape can be made very easily. (*See Illustration 31*)

NB: All the loose blades are interchangeable, so that Laces A to E can be repeated with different cut-out holes, giving quite a variety of effects.

Variations on the lace (*See Illustration 6*)

There are many possible variations on the lace theme as you will see on going through this book. This illustration shows a few, and the effect of colour.

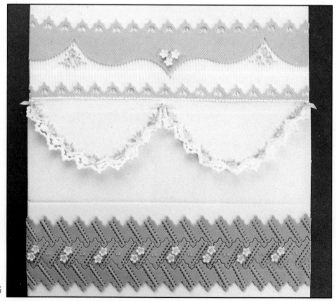

6

How to make the Borders (*See Illustration 7*)

Border A. 1. Fit the Straight Blade (LA2A) into any of the holes numbered 2 to 5 in the Border Body (LB1). This sets the width of the piece – from $7/8$" to $2^1/8$".

Then fit the 'Heart' blade (LA2B) inside the Straight Blade into any of the holes numbered 1 to 4.

2. Roll out the 'lace paste', not too thinly (for a collar use pastillage, see recipe Page 40), and press the assembled cutter firmly onto the paste. **Run your fingers along the top of the cutter** to make sure the holes are all cut properly. **DO NOT** scrub or twist the cutter. Lift straight up and then, if a longer piece is required, move the cutter along, line up carefully with the previous cut and press down and lift up as before. Cut to the exact length required and peel away the surplus material.

NB: For ease of handling, strips of about 10" – 12" long are the most convenient. For longer pieces butt the ends of the strips together when applying to the cake.

3. Then lift the Lace piece off the board **with the cut-outs still in place***, moisten with a little water and attach to the cake in the required position. Carefully push out the cut-outs with a cocktail stick just before the paste begins to harden. For a collar, leave to dry before placing on the cake.

If you intend to stand it upright, use paste glue (see Page 40) for greater strength and an invisible join!

*This helps to reduce any tendency of the piece to distort or stretch.

Border B. 1. For a border with a shaped edge on both sides leave out the Straight Blade (LA2A) and, after Step 2 of Border A, position the shaped edge of the Border Body Cutter (LB1) a little below the holes you have just cut, and cut again, running your fingers along the top of the blade'.

Border C. 1. As for Border B, but turn LB1 round.

Border D. 1. If several blades are fitted into LB1, then an attractive perforated drape can be made very easily.

Border E. 1. Equally, the small sets of hole cutters from the cut up blades (as mentioned in Item 3 Page 4) can be used by hand to make many interesting patterns (*See Illustration 5*).

NB: All the loose blades are interchangeable, so that Borders A to E can be repeated with different cut-out holes, giving quite a variety of effects.

How to make the Collars (*See Illustration 23 P.24*).

1. Cut out any of the Borders above in pastillage. Crimp or emboss them as required and leave to dry.

2. Attach to the top of the cake with **at least** a $1/4$" overlap, using paste glue.

3. Pipe or glue any further decorations as required. If there are any gaps between the collars, fill with a flower or butterfly.

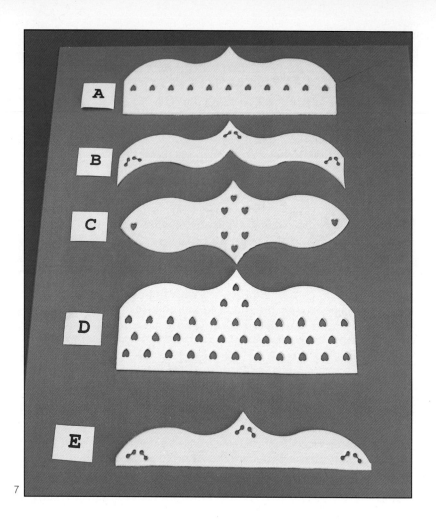

7

How to use the Lantern cutter (*See Illustration 36 P.32*).

1. Roll out Brown paste and cut out one Lantern shape, by pressing the cutter down and lifting up. Leave to dry.

2. Attach to the top or side of the cake with Royal Icing or paste glue. Decorate with flowers or paint a little yellow in the centre openings to represent a flame.

3. Use it to emboss a lantern shape on the side of a cake and pipe round with Dark Brown Royal Icing or paint in the shape with food colours.

4. Cut out 4 lanterns as above, cut off the top ring and assemble them as three dimensional lantern, glueing with paste glue.

5. It can even be used as a gazebo! See Cake 9, Page 28.

8

How to make the Honeysuckle (*See Illustration 8*).

1.Tape 1- long Green stamen and 5- Yellow shorter stamens together onto the end of a 33 gauge wire.

2. Press a ball of White flowerpaste into the 2nd smallest hole on the Mexican Hat Adaptor(M1), pull out and place on your non-stick board. Roll out the brim until it is petal thin.

3. Place your chosen Honeysuckle cutter(HS1,HS2 or HS3) over the 'hat' and cut out one petal. **DO NOT** scrub or twist the cutter. Peel away surplus material.(*See Illustration 9*)

4. Dip the Petal Veining Tool (OP2) in Trex and hollow out the centre of the flower. Press each of the petals gently against the tool with your finger to vein them. Widen the centre of the flower a little.

5. Place a touch of 'glue' on the base of the stamens and thread the wire through the centre of the flower.

6. Press gently round the base to shape the flower, but still keeping the 'cup' effect, then roll down between your two fingers to give a long trumpet. Curve the petals back to shape. Leave to dry.

7. When dry, dust with your chosen petal dust. There are many colours of honeysuckle.

8. The flowers are assembled in groups of 6 arranged in a circle.

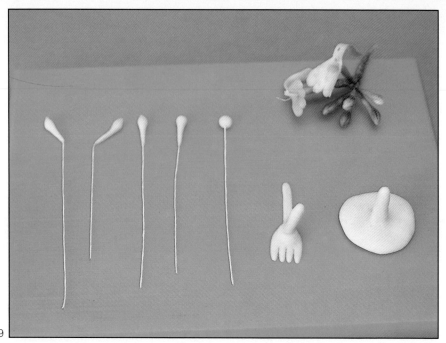

9

9.Bud. Moisten the end of a 30 gauge White wire with rose water and push into a small ball of White flowerpaste. Roll between your finger and thumb to form a cone shape. Continue rolling down the wire until it is a fine sausage shape. Mark the cone with a knife – 4 ridges on the top of each bud in the shape of a cross. Glue a small ball of Green paste at the base of each bud. Hold the wire at the base of the bud and bend over the top.

When dry, dust with colour of choice.

10. Tape together in groups of 12, two circles of 6.

11. Leaves are a long oval shape (See Template 9a). Roll out a sausage of Green flowerpaste and flatten. Mark one vein down the centre with the Veining Tool (OP2).

Template
9a

—12—

10

How to make the Butterflies (*See Illustration 10*).

1. Roll out White flowerpaste until it is transparent.

Cut the paste in half, following a **curved** line, and place the top half of the paste slightly overlapping the bottom half.

2. Press your chosen butterfly cutter down onto the paste so that the 'overlap' comes just above the lower half of the wing, and lift up. **DO NOT** twist or scrub the cutter. Leave to dry.

This is an easy way to give the usual four wings to the butterfly. B1 needs to be folded at the centre while still soft and supported.

3. When dry, dust both sides with petal dust on a soft brush to give the base colour.

4. Use a fine sable brush (000) and liquid colour to paint in the markings. To avoid uneven paint distribution, paint a little of the colour onto greaseproof paper and work it until smooth before applying to the butterfly wing.

5. An alternative method of marking is, having dusted, carefully scratch out the markings with a craft knife.

6. Pipe the head and body with Royal Icing, and, while still soft, carefully ease the wings into the sides of the body.

Support the wings with 'cloud drift' or bent cardboard.

7. Cut 2 fine stamens for the antennae, and press into the head while the icing is still soft. Leave to dry.

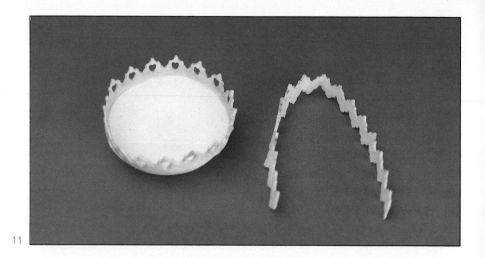

How to make the Lace Basket (*See Illustrations 11 & 12*).

1. Cut out a circle of pastillage (3–4" dia.) and leave to dry in a shallow cup, such as a poached egg container.

2. Cut out Lace A or B (9–12" long) and stick round the edge. When dry colour with petal dust.

3. Make a handle from Pastillage Lace C (no holes), length to suit your requirement, bend round a suitable support and, when dry, dust and stick to the basket with paste glue or Royal Icing.

13

How to make the Wedding Top (*See Illustration 13*).

1. Cut out Lace A 13$^{1}/_{2}$" long, stand on edge and make a circle 4$^{1}/_{2}$" inside dia.(shaped round a biscuit cutter or similar). Join the ends with paste glue. Repeat with a 4$^{1}/_{2}$" length and 1$^{1}/_{2}$" inside dia. circle. Leave to dry.

2. Cut out Lace B 10 holes long but **leave the hole cut-outs in place** so that it does not change shape as you bend it. Dust the Template 15 for the upright and bend the lace to the shape of the template. Remove the hole cut-outs carefully with a cocktail stick. Place a finger on each side of the hole shape while removing the cut-outs to keep the shape, and then leave to dry.

3. Repeat Step 2 nine times (includes two spares!).

4. Support the $1\frac{1}{2}$" dia. circle on a narrow topped cylinder 4" high(2 colour containers?), placed in the centre of the $4\frac{1}{2}$" dia. circle. Glue one of the uprights to the top and bottom circles with paste glue or Royal Icing. Support as required with empty film containers or similar.

5. Glue the second upright opposite to the first in the same way.(See Illustration 14).

6. Glue the next two uprights at right angles to the first two and leave to dry.

7. When dry, continue with the remaining four uprights placed symmetrically. If you are going to hang anything from the top, such as cut out bells, do this, after leaving 3 uprights to dry, **before** fitting the final upright. This reduces the risk of breakages.

8. When dry, petal dust if required, and decorate with leaves and blossoms to taste.

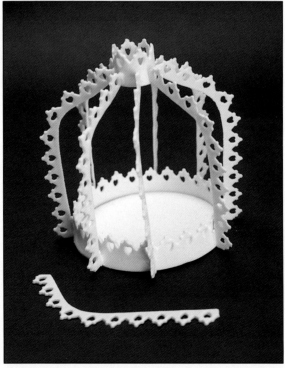

14

16

How to make the Pointed Dome (*See Illustration 16*).

1.Make a circle of Lace A 4¹/₂" dia., stood on edge, glue the ends together and leave to dry.

2. Cut out Lace B 16 holes long, but **leave the hole cut-outs in place** so that it does not change shape as you bend it. Dust the Template 17 for the upright and bend the lace to the shape of the template. Remove the hole cut-outs carefully with a cocktail stick. Place a finger on each side of the hole shape while removing the cut-outs to keep the shape and then leave to dry.

3. Repeat Step 2 nine times (includes two spares!).

4. Place a narrow topped support (such as a paste bottle with a piece of sponge on top), 4¹/₄" high, in the centre of the circle from Step 1. Place two of the uprights opposite to each other and glue to each other and to the base circle with paste glue or Royal Icing. They will need careful support at the sides.

I do not recommend joining them when placed flat and then lifting into position.

5. Repeat for the two uprights at right angles to the first two and leave to dry.

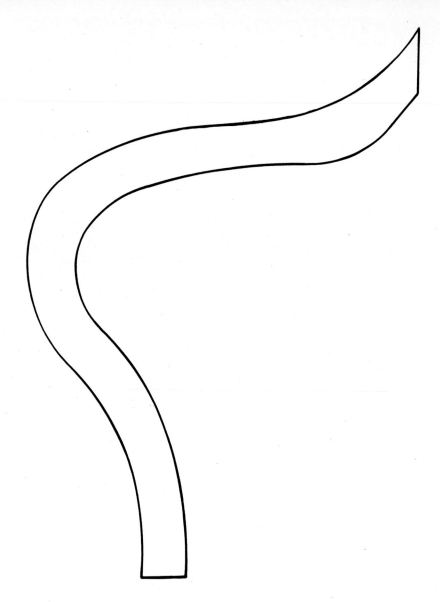

Template
17

6. When dry glue the remaining 4 uprights into position symmetrically. If you are going to hang anything from the top, such as cut out bells or the Baby's Mobile, do this, after leaving 3 uprights to dry, **before** fitting the final upright. This reduces the risk of breakages.

7. Petal dust and decorate with leaves and blossoms as required.

How to make the Baby's Mobile (*See Illustration 16*).

1. Make a template of the teddy bear as Template 18 out of plastic from a food or ice cream container.

2. Roll out flowerpaste, dust the template with cornflour and cut out the shape. With the template still in position rub round the edge with your finger to remove the cut look.

3. An alternative method is to lay the template on the rolled out flowerpaste and roll over with a rolling pin. Remove the template and cut round the impression in the paste.

4. Make a small hole in the top of the teddy with a cocktail stick to thread the cotton through.

5. Leave to dry on a cornflour dusted board. When dry, outline in Brown with a paintbrush.

6. Cut out star shapes, put a hole in the top and leave to dry.

7. Cut out two Lace B strips 7 holes long and leave to dry. Paint rainbow colours on both sides. Tie a cotton thread to the centre of each strip and hang 3 or 4 of the cut-out shapes from each one with cotton thread. Balance each strip separately before trying to assemble.

8. Assemble the two strips at their centres, one under the other at right angles. Check the height of the mobile(you have 4" clear space) and then attach carefully to the centre of the pointed dome.

Template
18

The Lace Cakes.

This section shows a variety of complete cakes using the lace pieces, to give you ideas for your own creations. The detailed descriptions will normally only refer to the lace work.

The Drape. Roll out Lace Paste thinly on a dusted board 2" larger than the top of the cake. Trim round the edge. Place the board over the cake and slide the drape across the surface. Neaten the folds by lifting with your finger under the edge at positions N, S, E & W and two positions in between. Leave to dry.

19

Cake 1.(*See Illustration 19*) Cover the cake and board with Peach sugarpaste. Crimp the board edge. Leave to dry. Cover the top of the cake with a Cream paste drape as above.

Cut strips of White Lace A, Straight edge (LA2A) in holes 5, hole cut out (LA2B) in holes 2. Cut another row of holes close to the edge as for Lace B. Crimp a line along the strip between the holes.

Attach to the side of the cake with paste glue, balancing on your hand(as for a Garrett Frill)and ease paste onto the folds of the drape.

Smooth the join between strips with the balling tool (OP1). Leave to dry.

Cut out strip of Lace B, crimp the straight edge and glue around the top edge of the cake to conceal the join.

Cut out strip of Lace B and paste glue it, on edge, in a circle on the top of the cake.

Tip: For the last step, place a round board on top of the cake as a guide. Leave a piece of paste or similar in the centre of the board so that you can remove it easily!

The top decoration also includes the idea of making numerals (or letters) from the lace. Just bend over the shape of your favourite type face.

Cake 2. (*See Illustration 20*)

Cover the cake and the board with Peach sugarpaste, leaving a $\frac{1}{2}$" gap round the edge of the board. Leave to dry.

Cut out strip of Lace B. Stick round the base with water/paste glue, straight onto the board. Pipe dots all round the join.

Roll out lace paste and cut out a square drape (see Page 20), using a square board as a template. When dry, cut out four strips of Lace B and attach to the edges of the square with water or paste glue. Pipe a snail trail round the joins and finish the cake with a little embroidery piped with Royal Icing.

Cake 3. (*See Illustration 21*)

Cover the cake and board with Brown sugarpaste. Leave to dry.

Make a circular Cream sugarpaste drape (see Page 20). Cut out strips of Lace B with the Straight Edge (LA2A) in holes 3. Frill the straight edge with a Frilling Tool and attach with a little water around the base edge of the drape with the lace facing down. Butt the ends of the strips together.

Attach a similar Lace B around the base of the cake with the lace edge standing up.

22

Cake 4. (*See Illustration 22*)

Cover the cake and board with Brown sugarpaste. Leave to dry. Cut out a circle of Cream Lace paste 2" larger diameter than the cake and place on top. Cut out 5 plain Borders A with the Straight Blade(LA2A) in Holes 2. Omit the hole blade. Attach the Borders to the edge of the top circle with paste glue,

When dry, cut out strips of Lace B and attach round the top edge of the cake to cover the joins.

Cut out strips of Lace B and paste glue it, on edge, in a circle on the top of the cake.(See tip on Page 20).

23

Cake 5. (*See Illustration 23*) **6" square**.

Cover the cake and board with Brown sugarpaste.

Cut out 4 pastillage Borders for the collars, fitting the Straight Blade (LA2A) into holes 2 in body (LB1). Leave to dry.

For the base, cut out 4 Borders using holes 1.

For the side decoration cut out lengths of Lace D, including the holes, and attach with a little water or glue.

Decorate with an open rose and leaves on top (see Book 1) and butterflies (B4) on each of the corners (see Page 14). Pipe embroidery on the borders, and a snail trail of Royal Icing round the base and top of the borders.

24

25

Cake 6. (*See Illustration 24*)

Cover the cake and board with Cream sugarpaste. Emboss a pattern round the base with a Daphne cutter (D1).

Make 8 Garrett Frills in White and Brown sugarpaste (see Book 3), and attach to the sides.

Cut 8 lengths of Lace B, using holes 1, and attach round the cake on top of the frills with a little water or glue.

Add an open rose with leaves(see Book 1) and pipe Royal Icing in embroidery patterns, if required.

Cake 7. *(See Illustration 25)*

Cover the cake and board with Cream sugarpaste.

Emboss a pattern round the base with a Daisy cutter (DY8).

Cut out 6 pieces of Lace B, using holes 2, in Peach and attach diagonally to the sides of the cake with a little water or glue.

Cut out 6 pieces of Lace D, using holes 1, in Cream and attach to the sides of the cake overlapping the Peach lace pieces.

Finish the side decoration with small piped dots of Brown Royal Icing. The top decorations are the Maidenhair Fern and Daisies (see Book 6).

Cake 8. *(See Illustration 26).* **5" Hexagonal cake.**

Cover the cake in Coffee coloured sugarpaste and the board in White.

Cut out 3 - Border A in White with the Straight Edge Blade(LA2A) in Holes 3, and the Hole Blade(LA2C) in holes 1. Crimp a pattern along the straight edge and attach to the side of the cake with a little water or glue.

When dry, pipe a snail trail along the top edge and place a ribbon round the base.

Cut out strips of Lace B and attach on edge round the edge of the board with paste glue.

The top decorations are the Maidenhair Fern and Daisies (see Book 6).

28

29

Cake 9. (*See Illustrations 27 – 29*)

This simple idea uses coloured sugarpaste pieces cut out with the lace cutters and various other leaf cutters to form a country scene. The cutters used were the lace cutters, honeysuckle, lantern, maple leaf, oak leaf, and holly. Enjoy sorting out which does what. The top of the lantern cutter makes the gazebo!

30

Cake 10. (*See Illustration 30*)

This design is displayed on a perspex 'Swan' cake stand. It illustrates the drape edged with a Garrett Frill, with an overlap of Lace D trimmed with pearls. It also shows how easily the lace strip can be curled round on top of the cake to give a very attractive and unusual effect. Sprays of honeysuckle to finish.

Cake 11. (*See Illustration 31*)

This idea uses a fabric covered board and strips of White Lace E with holes 1, 3 & 5 used, and rows 2 & 4 put in by hand, staggered. The holes are painted or dusted in different colours.

A strips of Lace C finish off the top edge, and the top decoration is the Lace Cradle from Page 35.

31

32

Cake 12. (*See Illustration 32*)

This heart shaped cake uses White Lace C overlapping with Mauve Garrett Frills.

The top decorations are Quick Crane's-bill, Wood Anemone flowers and three butterflies. See Pages 36,38 & 13,

Cake 13. (*See Illustrations 33 – 35*)

These close-ups show how the lace strip can be used as a bridge for different styles of extension work.

33

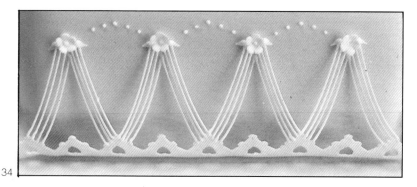

34

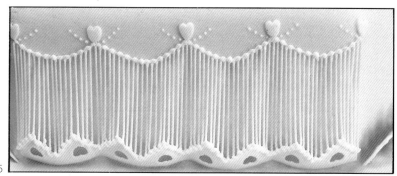

35

36

37

Cake 14. (*See Illustrations 36 & 37*)

The Lantern cake gives an effective top design using poinsettias(see Page 36).

It also shows an interesting side design, using a plaque cutter(P3) to cut a hole in the outer skin of sugarpaste to give added depth to the arrangement of three dimensional flowers.

38

How to make the Lace Horseshoe *(See Illustration 38)*

1. Cut out a 9" length of Lace B with the Straight Edge (LA2A) in holes 2. Bend to shape and leave to dry.

2. Decorate as required.

39

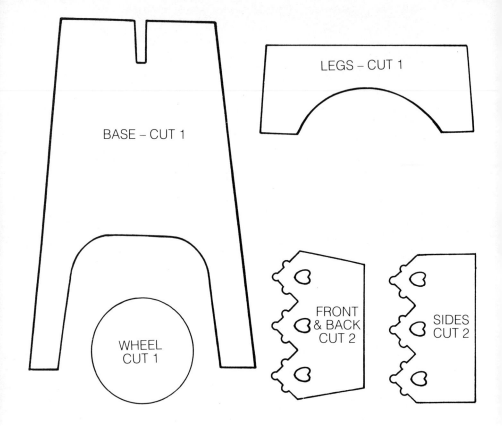

BASE – CUT 1

LEGS – CUT 1

WHEEL
CUT 1

FRONT
& BACK
CUT 2

SIDES
CUT 2

40

How to make the Lace Wheelbarrow (*See Illustration 39*).

1. Make some plastic or cardboard templates for the base, leg and wheel of the wheelbarrow as shown in Illustration 40.

2. Roll our White pastillage fairly thickly(3mm) and cut out 1 - base, 1 - leg, 1 -wheel 1" dia., and 4 - pieces of Lace A, each 3 holes long. Cut the ends of two pieces of the lace at an angle as shown in Illustration 40. Leave to dry.

3. Make sure the wheel will fit easily into the slot in the front of the base.

4. Attach the lace pieces to the base with Royal Icing or paste glue, with the tapered pieces at the front and back, inside the side pieces.

5. When dry, turn over the wheelbarrow and attach the leg and wheel with Royal Icing.

6. When dry, fill with sugar flowers, such as mini roses, blossoms or fruits.

41

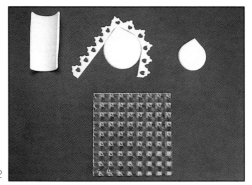

42

How to make the Lace Cradle (*See Illustration 41*).

1. Roll out White flowerpaste or pastillage to medium thickness (about 2mm) and cut out Rose Petals, 1 - large (R1) and 1 - medium (R2), and a rectangle of paste 2" x 1$^1/_2$" (50 x 38mm).

Decorate the petals by cutting holes with a single 'Heart' cutter.

2.Place the rectangle over a 1"(25mm) dia. rolling pin or former, lengthways, and leave all items to dry.

3. Using 'lace paste' or pastillage, cut out a strip of Lace B(see Page 8), using holes 1 ($^7/_8$") illustrated, or any other style you wish. Moisten the edges of the petals(R1 & R2) with rose water, and bend and stick the lace strip round the petals, making sure one of the decorative holes is at the top. Trim surplus and leave to dry. (*See Illustration 42*).

3. When dry, if required, pipe coloured Royal Icing round the edges or use petal dust. Apply any other painted decoration before assembling.

4. Fit the two ends and the body together with piped stiff Royal Icing, and decorate further, if required, with small flowers (or hearts!), and/or ribbons.

5. The quilt is made by pressing the sheet of dimpled plastic onto soft sugarpaste, and painting when dry. (*See Illustration 42*).

How to make the Quick Crane's-bill (Herb-robert)
(See Illustrations 43 & 44). by Alan Dunn.

1. Pistil. Tape a small flap of White florist's tape onto a 28 gauge wire. Cut the flap into five.

2. Tape 10 short stamens onto a 28 gauge wire. Colour the tips Black. Then tape round the pistil.

3. Push a piece of White flowerpaste into the smallest hole on the Mexican Hat Adaptor (M1), roll out the brim and cut out a five-petal flower (F9). Soften the edges on the Orchard Pad and cup slightly with a balling tool(OP1). Vein the petals with the Petal Veining Tool (OP2).

4. Thread the stamens through the centre of the flower and hang upside down on the Flower Stand (S1) to dry slightly.

5. Roll out Green flowerpaste and cut a calyx(R13A). Soften the edges, apply a little rose water to the base of the flower and thread the calyx onto the back. Allow to dry.

6. Apply a little Green petal dust to the centre of the flower. Dust the edges with some Violet and Cornflower Blue on both the back and front.

Leaves. 7. Roll out some Green flowerpaste, leaving the centre slightly thicker. Cut out a large Japanese Maple Leaf (JM1).

8. Broaden each segment, using a cocktail stick or Frilling tool.

9. Dip the end of a 28 gauge wire into rose water and, holding the leaf firmly between finger and thumb, insert the wire into the leaf.

10. Press onto a veiner or a real leaf, or mark the veins with the Petal Veining Tool(OP2). Then, using a scalpel or scissors, cut out small 'V' shapes round the edge.

11. Gently soften with a Balling tool (OP1) and allow to dry.

12. Make the flower in varying sizes, using F7, F8 and F10.

How to make the Poinsettia (See Illustration 45 & 46)

1. Roll our Red flowerpaste and cut out 1 – Six petal flower (N2). Ball from the tip to the centre along each petal. Mark one vein down the centre with the Petal Veining Tool (OP2).

2. Repeat Step 1 for Petals N3 and N4.

3. Stick the flowers on top of each other with rose water, smallest on top, interleaving the petals.

4. Pipe a bulb of Green Royal Icing in the centre and pipe Yellow dots on top.

43

44

45

46

47

48

How to make the Wood Anemone (*See Illustrations 47 & 48*).

1. Place a small ball of Light Green paste on the end of a 30 gauge wire, and pop in about 30 Yellow stamen heads. Leave to dry.

2. Roll out White flowerpaste and cut out 1 – N4 Six Petal Flower (or any of the sizes will do). Widen the base of each petal with the balling tool (OP1) and vein it with the Petal Veining Tool (OP2).

3. Cup the flower in the centre and thread the stamen wire through.

When dry, dust a streak of Pale Mauve down the back of the petals.

4. Roll out Green flowerpaste and cut out 1 – Maple Leaf (JM1). Cut up into sections as in the illustration, to form the leaves. Stroke the sides of the leaves with an anger tool and vein them with the Petal Veining Tool (OP2). Glue a 33 gauge wire into each of the leaves.

5. When dry, wire each section of leaf together (three segments). Tape the single flower above the leaves.

6. The Bud is cone shaped with 6 indentations around. Dust with Pale Mauve.

7. The fruiting head is a Pale Green ball of paste on a 30 gauge wire. Stick tiny Green cones to the ball with rose water.

— 38 —

RECIPES

Lace Paste A.

250g($^1/_2$ lb) Bakels' Pettinice' or Craigmillars Pastello' **only.**

1 teaspoon(5ml)Gum Tragacanth.

Rub Trex on your hands and knead ingredients together until elastic. Wrap tightly in plastic and store in an airtight container. Leave for 24 hours. There is no need to refrigerate. This paste keeps well if worked through, say, once a week. Always keep tightly wrapped.

Flowerpaste D.

450g (1lb) sieved icing sugar

5mls Gum Tragacanth and 20mls

Carboxymethylcellulose (CMC)

10mls powdered Gelatine soaked in 25mls cold water

10mls white fat (Trex or Spry, not lard)

10mls liquid Glucose

45mls egg white

Sieve all the icing sugar into a **greased*** (Trex) mixing bowl. Add the gums to the sugar. Warm the mixture in a microwave oven 3x50 secs on a medium setting, stirring in between.

Sprinkle the gelatine over the water in a cup and allow to 'sponge'. Put the cup in hot,not boiling water,until clear. Add the white fat and liquid glucose. Heat the 'K' or Dough hook beater, add the dissolved ingredients and the egg white to the warmed sugar, and beat on the lowest speed until all the ingredients are combined. At this stage the mixture will be a dingy beige colour. Turn the machine to maximum speed and mix until the mixture becomes white and stringy. Grease your hands and remove the paste from the machine. Pull and stretch the paste several times. Knead together and cut into 4 sections. Knead each section again and place in a plastic bag, then in an airtight container and keep in the refrigerator. Let it mature for 24 hours. This paste dries quickly so, when ready to use, cut off only a very small piece and re-seal the remainder. Work it well with your fingers. It should 'click' between your fingers when ready to use. If it should be a little too hard and crumbly, add a little egg white and fat. The fat slows down the drying process and the egg white makes it more pliable.

Keep coloured paste in separate container. This paste keeps for several months.

* This eases the strain on the machine considerably.

Pastillage C.

Make up 8ozs Royal Icing. Add two teaspoons Tylose. Mix thoroughly. Wrap in cling film and put into an airtight container. Leave 24 hrs before working.

Paste Glue.

1oz sugarpaste of the same colour as the items to be glued.

2 dessertspoons of warm water

Gradually combine together and place in the microwave oven for 1 $-1^1/_2$ mins until the mixture boils. When cool use as required. Store at room temperature, or refrigerate if not to be used for a length of time.

If the glue is to be used immediately then it is not necessary to boil it.